Tiger Time 1

STUDENT'S BOOK

My name is ______________________.

macmillan education

Carol Read • Mark Ormerod

Tiger Time 1 Syllabus

	Active vocabulary	Active structures	CLIL
Hello, Tiger!	hello, goodbye roar, jump, run, tiger boy, girl, colours, numbers 1–10 apple, ball, banana, book, cat, dog raining, cold, sunny, windy, cloudy, hot	What's your name? I'm (Tiger). How old are you? I'm (six). How many (tigers)? It's (hot).	
1 Back to School	bag, pencil, pen, crayon, ruler, rubber, pencil case, sharpener talk, draw, colour, play, sing	Can I have this (pencil), please? Yes, of course. Put it in the basket. I (draw) at school. Do you (sing) at school? Yes, I do./No, I don't. My school uniform is (blue).	Social Science: What we do at school
2 The Gingerbread Man	head, eyes, mouth, nose, ears, arms, hands, legs listen, smell, see, touch, taste	I've got (arms). This is (the head). This is my (nose). I (see) with my (eyes). We play (tag).	Science: Our five senses
3 Tiger is Lost	father, mother, brother, grandmother, grandfather, sister, baby, family aunt, uncle, cousin, small, big	Have you got (Tiger)? Yes, I have./No, I haven't. This family is (big). Who's this? This is my (cousin). I live with (my mum and my brother).	Social Science: Different families
4 Dinner Time	peas, eggs, mushrooms, milk, carrots, potatoes, cheese, sausages numbers 1–20 plants, animals, fruit, vegetables, meat, fish	I love/like/don't like (beef). Do you like (cheese)? Yes, I do./No, I don't. Put (carrots) in the omelette. (Bananas) are (fruit). (Bananas) are from (plants). (Beef) is (meat). (Beef) is from animals.	Science: Food we eat
5 The Sore Paw	parrot, snake, elephant, monkey, giraffe, frog, crocodile, mouse walk, run, climb, jump, swim, fly	I've got a sore (paw). Can you help me, please? No, sorry. I can't./Yes, of course I can. A (giraffe) can (run). I can (jump). Can you (fly)? Yes, I can./No, I can't. I can see a (mouse). It's (brown).	Science: How we move
6 The Missing Skateboard	car, doll, bike, scooter, skateboard, kite, board game, computer game wood, plastic, metal, paper	Where's my (skateboard)? Is it in/on/under the (table)? Yes, it is./No, it isn't. The (car) is in/on/under the (book). My (pencil) is made of (wood). In the holidays, I play with my (bike).	Science: Materials
Festivals	**Mother's Day:** basket, bracelet, card, flower, present **Father's Day:** book, cake, football, hat, tie **Teacher's Day:** bag, mug, plant, sunflower, T-shirt	Have you got a basket? Yes, I have. I've got a yellow basket. Happy Mother's Day! I've got a present. It's for my dad. What is it? It's a (football). Happy Father's Day! What's your name? Have you got a (sunflower)? Yes, I have. Happy Teacher's Day!	

Hello, Tiger!

Lesson 1

1 Listen, point and mime. digital

2 ♫ Listen and sing *Hello, I'm Tiger*.

3 Make the Tiger mask (TB, p159). ♫ Act out the song.

Introduction and review: *I'm (Tiger). hello, goodbye, tiger, roar, jump, run, black, orange*

Lesson 2

4 CD1 5 Listen and sing *What's your name?* Say.

5 CD1 6 Listen. Answer the questions. Repeat.

6 Do a role play.

Introduction and review: *What's your name? I'm (Sue). How old are you? I'm (six). boy, girl,* numbers 1–10

Lesson 3

7 CD1 7 Listen, point and say *The colour chant*. Colour.

8 Find, trace and say the numbers. CD1 8 Listen, look and count.

Lesson 4

9 Listen, number and repeat.

a

b

c

d

e

f

10 Look and draw. Say.

1

2

3

Review: *It's (hot). raining, cold, sunny, windy, cloudy, hot*

1 Back to School

Lesson 1 Vocabulary

1 CD1 12 **Listen, look and repeat.** digital

2 CD1 13 **Listen, point and say *Tiger's word chant*.**

3 **Stick and say. Play *Word or number*.**

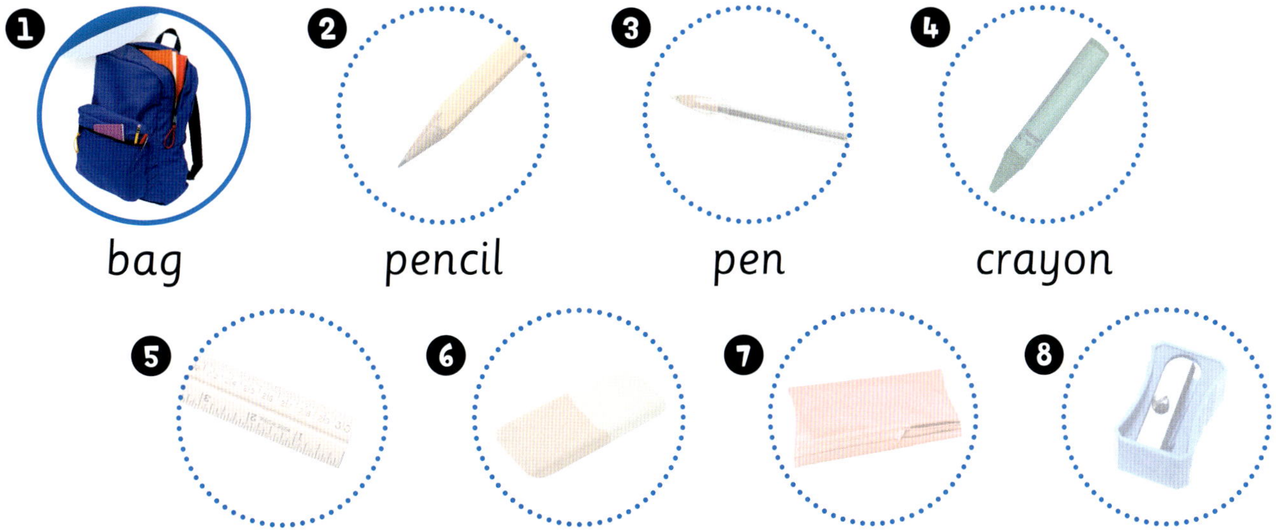

1 bag
2 pencil
3 pen
4 crayon
5 ruler
6 rubber
7 pencil case
8 sharpener

Vocabulary input: *bag, pencil, pen, crayon, ruler, rubber, pencil case, sharpener*

Lesson 2 Story

digital

4 CD1 14 Listen to the story. Say *stop!* Answer the questions.

Story and language input: *Can I have this (pencil), please? Yes, of course.*

Tiger Values

When you ask for something, say 'please' and 'thank you'.

Personal response and values

Lesson 3 Story activities

5 Listen and say the missing words.

6 Circle the things Sue and Jay buy.

1

2

3

4
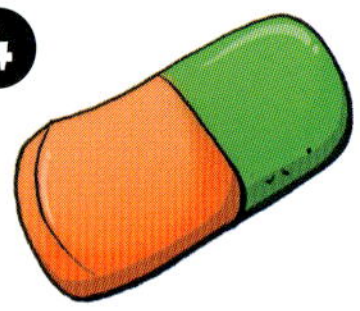

5

6

7

8

7 Listen and sing *Can I have this pen, please?*

Find, colour and say.

Lesson 4 Speaking

8 Listen, look and say.

9 Make the cut-out on page 83. Act out the story.

10 Do a role play.

Pronunciation: *Put the pen and the pencil in the pencil case.*
Communication: *Can I have this (pen), please? Yes, of course. Put it in the basket.*

SOCIAL SCIENCE

What we do at school

Lesson 5 CLIL

11 CD1 19 **Listen and point. Mime and say.**

1 

2 

3 

4 

5 

12 CD1 20 **Listen and repeat. Answer the questions.**

PING AND PONG

Content input: what we do at school: *talk, draw, colour, play, sing*

Lesson 6 CLIL

SOCIAL SCIENCE

13 CD1 21 Listen, number and repeat.

14 CD1 22 Listen and point. Sing *I draw at school*.

Tick (✓) what you do at school.

a

✓

b

c

1

d

e

OVER TO YOU

15 Play *Mime and guess*.

Content and personalisation: *I (draw) at school. Do you (sing) at school? Yes, I do./No, I don't.*

Lesson 7 Unit review

16 CD1 23 **Listen, number and repeat. Read and stick.**

a

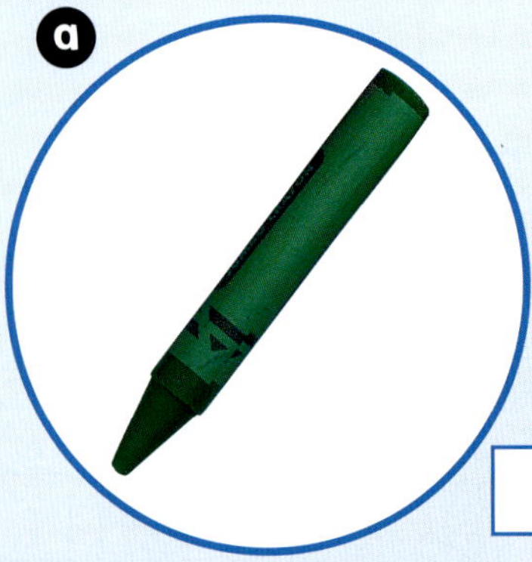

crayon

b

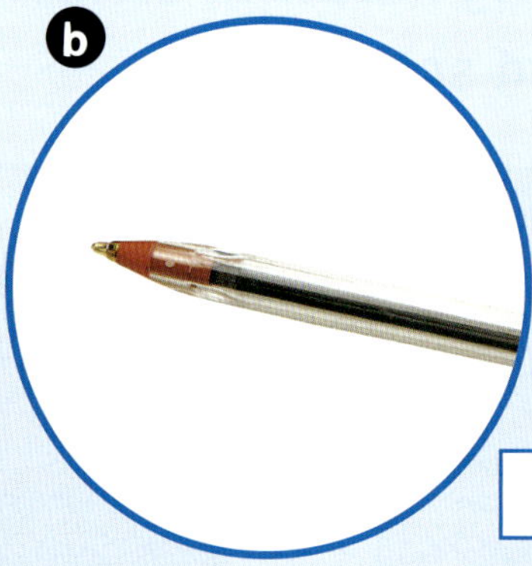

pen

c

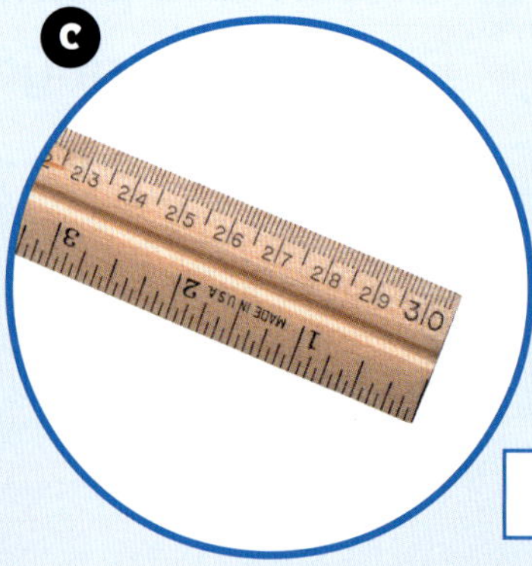

ruler

d

bag

e

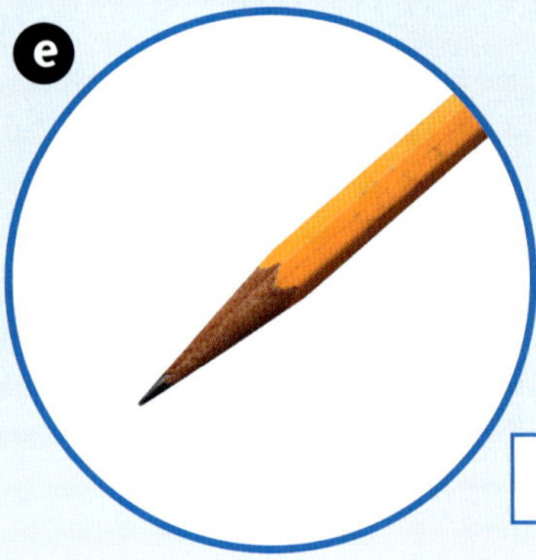

pencil

f

pencil case

g

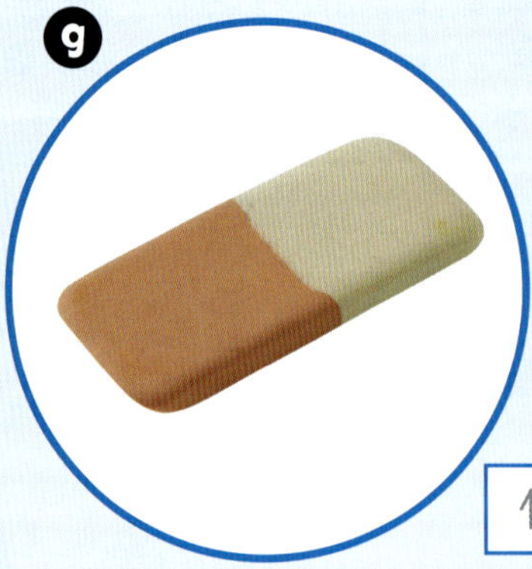

1

rubber

h

sharpener

17 Match and say.

18 CD1 24 Listen, point and repeat. Ask and answer.

CLASS CHAT

Learning to LEARN

Go to the Picture Dictionary on page 80.

Kids' Culture 1

1 CD1 25 Listen and say a traditional rhyme: ***Two, four, six, eight*.**

video

COMPARING CULTURES

2 CD1 26 Listen and number. Draw and say.

a

b

c

Intercultural learning: *Two, four, six, eight*
Language input: *My school uniform is (blue).*

2 The Gingerbread Man

Lesson 1 Vocabulary

1 CD1 29 Listen, look and repeat. digital

2 CD1 30 Listen, point and say *Tiger's word chant*.

3 Stick and say. Play *Word or number*.

1  head

2 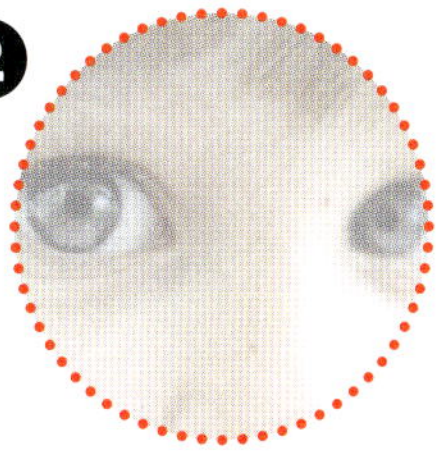 eyes

3 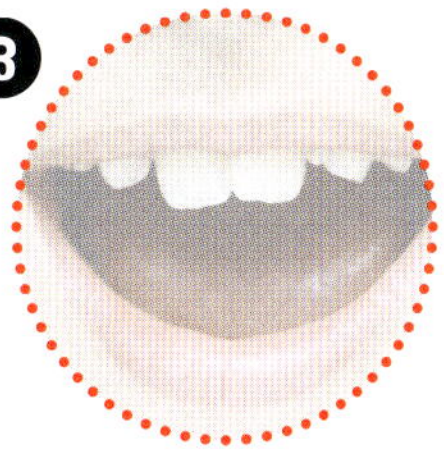 mouth

4 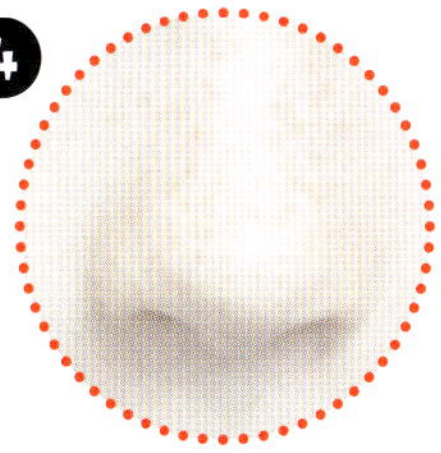 nose

5 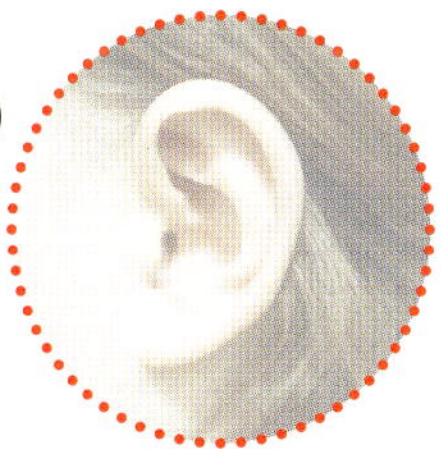 ears

6 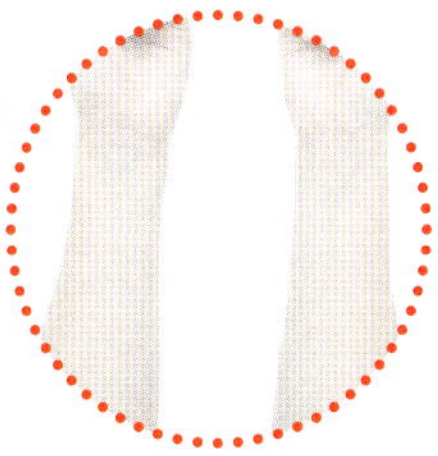 arms

7 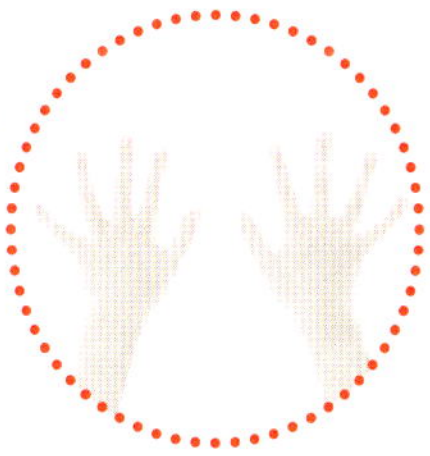 hands

8 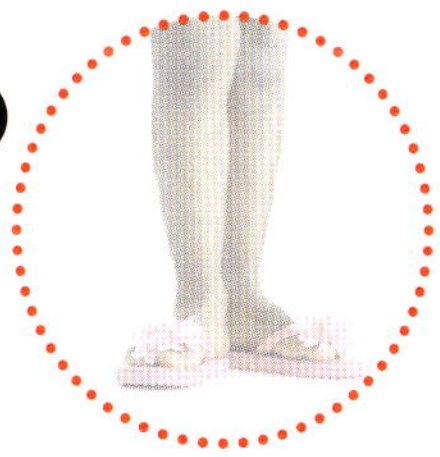 legs

Vocabulary input: *head, eyes, mouth, nose, ears, arms, hands, legs*

2 Lesson 2 Story

digital

4 CD1 31 **Listen to the story. Say *stop!* Answer the questions.**

STORYTIME

Story and language input: *I've got (arms). This is (the head).*

Tiger Values

Wash your hands before you touch food.

Lesson 3 Story activities

5 CD1 32 Listen and say the missing words.

6 Trace and colour. Point and say.

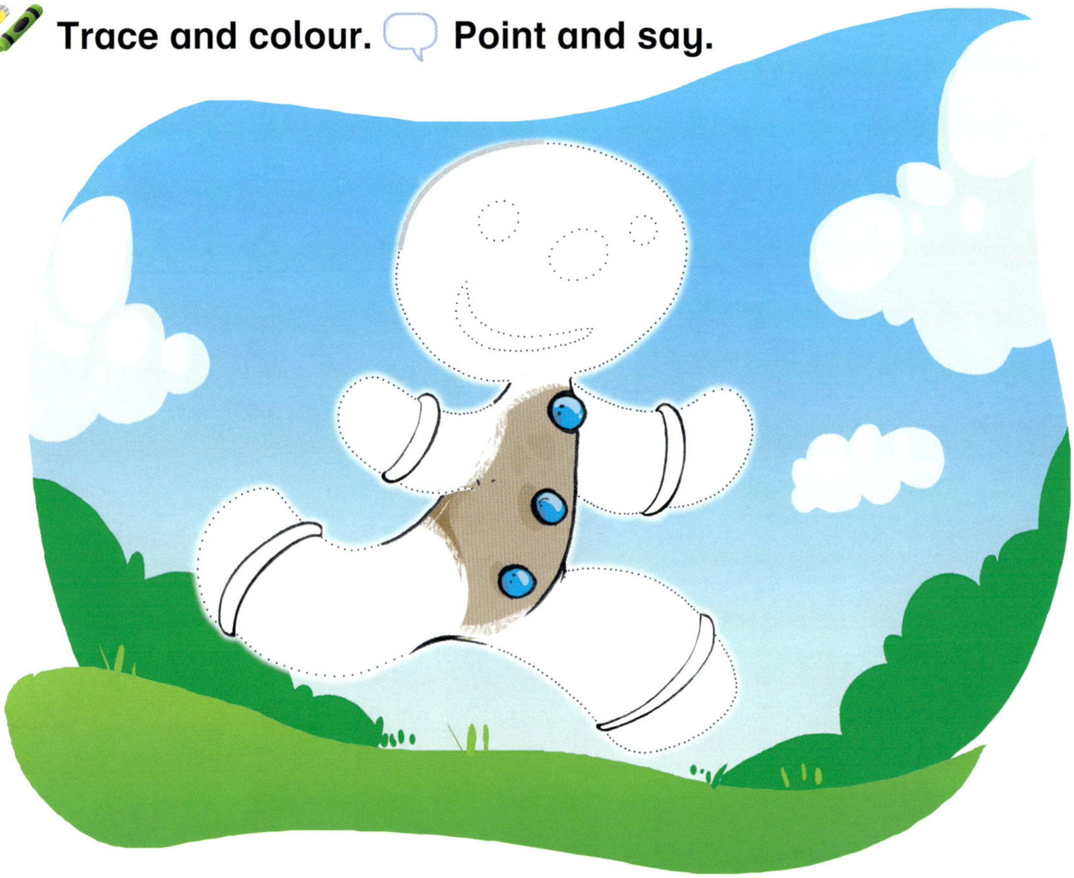

7 CD1 33 Listen and sing *I've got a head*.

Circle the gingerbread man from the story.

1

2

3

4

5

6

Lesson 4 Speaking

8 CD1 35 Listen, look and say.

9 Make the cut-out on page 85. Act out the story.

10 Play *This is my head!*

Pronunciation: *I've got a nose, but I've got no toes!*
Communication: *This is my (head).*

SCIENCE

Our five senses

Lesson 5 CLIL

11 CD1 36 Listen and point. Mime and say.

12 CD1 37 Listen and repeat. Answer the questions.

PING AND PONG

Content input: our five senses: *listen, smell, see, touch, taste*

Lesson 6 CLIL

SCIENCE

13 CD1 38 Listen, number and repeat.

14 CD1 39 Listen and point. Sing *I listen with my ears*. Match.

a

b

1

c

d

e

15 Play *I smell with my nose.*

Lesson 7 Unit review

16 CD1 40 **Listen, number and repeat. Read and stick.**

a
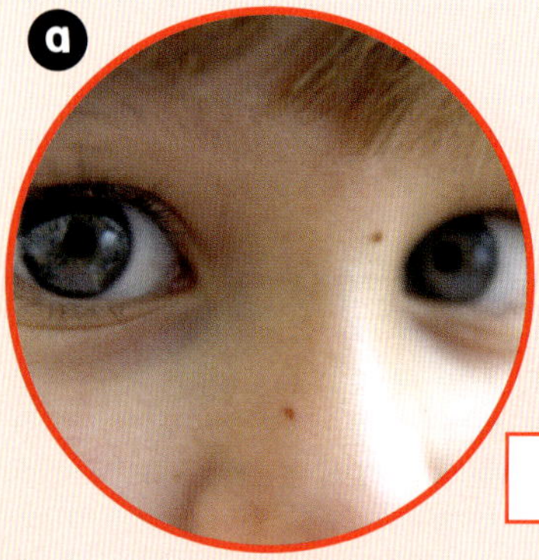
☐
eyes

b

1
head

c
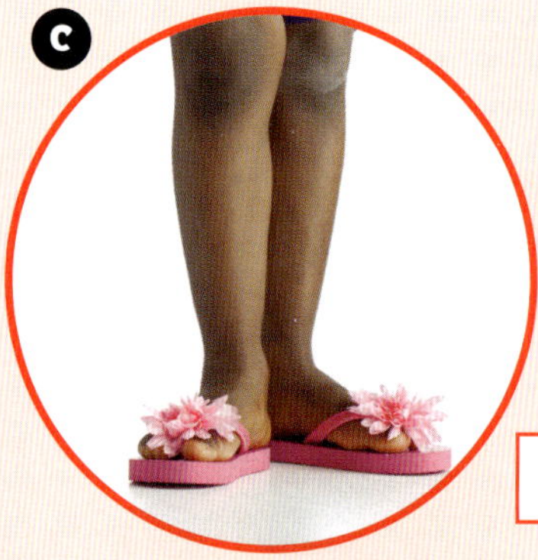
☐
legs

d
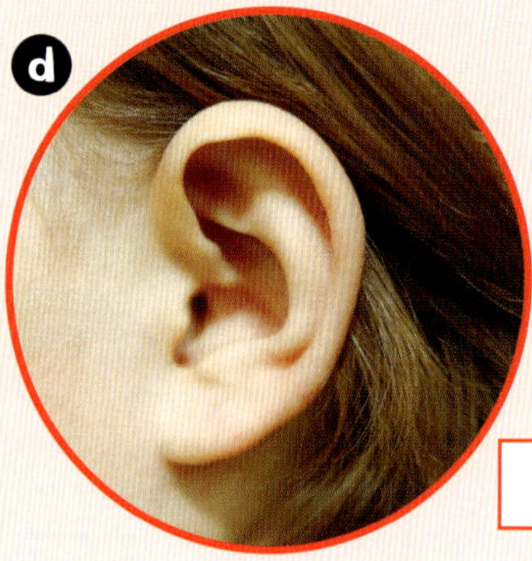
☐
ears

e
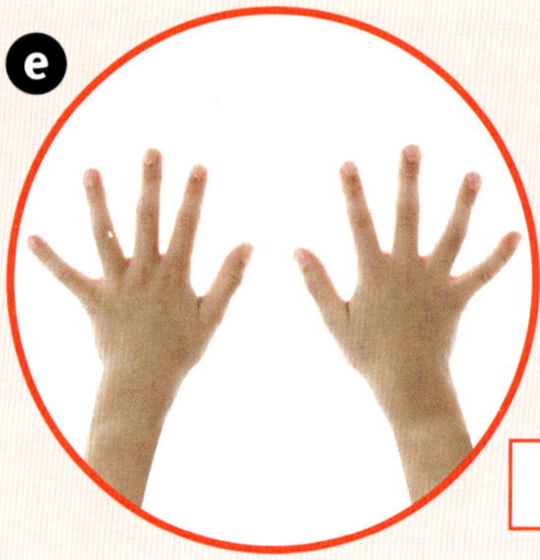
☐
hands

f
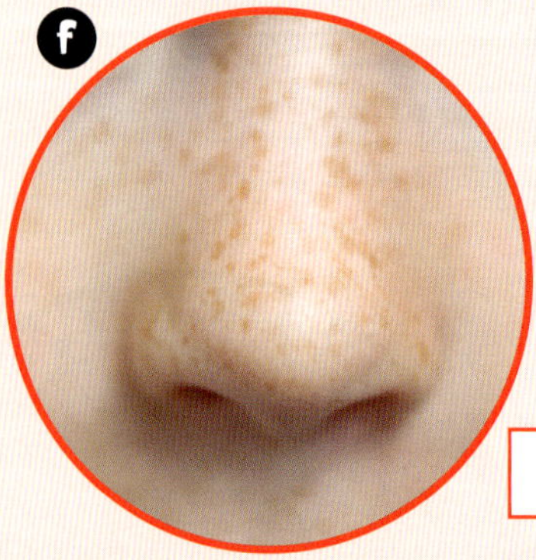
☐
nose

g
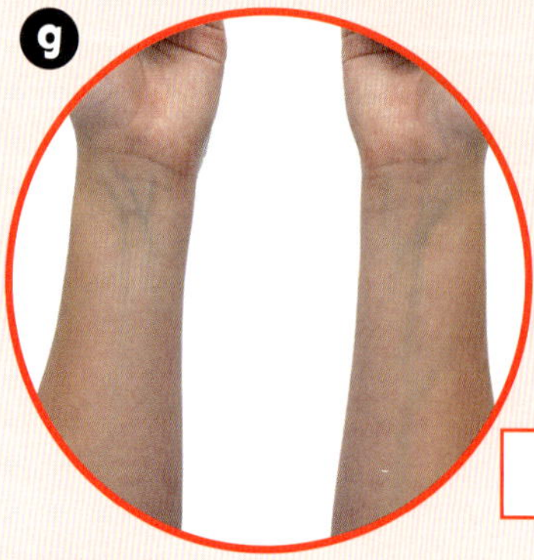
☐
arms

h
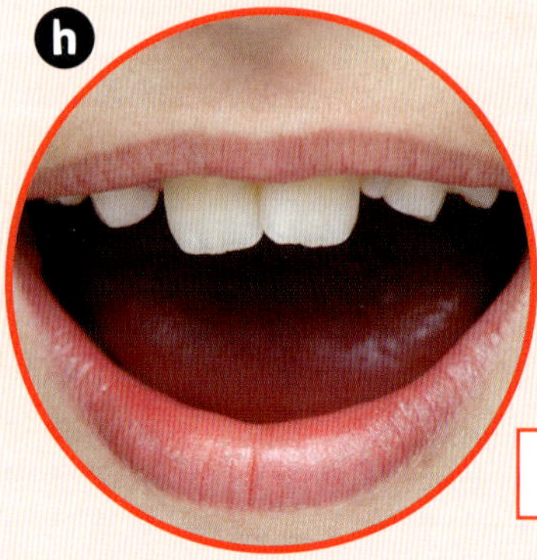
☐
mouth

17 Match and say.

CLASS CHAT

18 CD1 41 Listen and point. Listen again and respond.

Learning to LEARN

Go to the Picture Dictionary on page 80.

Kids' Culture 2

1 CD1 42 Listen, sing and act out a song: *Hokey cokey*.

video

2 CD1 43 Listen and number. Draw and say.

a

b

c

Intercultural learning: song: *Hokey cokey*
Language input: *We play (tag).*

Tiger Review 1

1 Play *Tiger says.*

2 CD1 44 Listen, number and say. Circle red or blue.

a

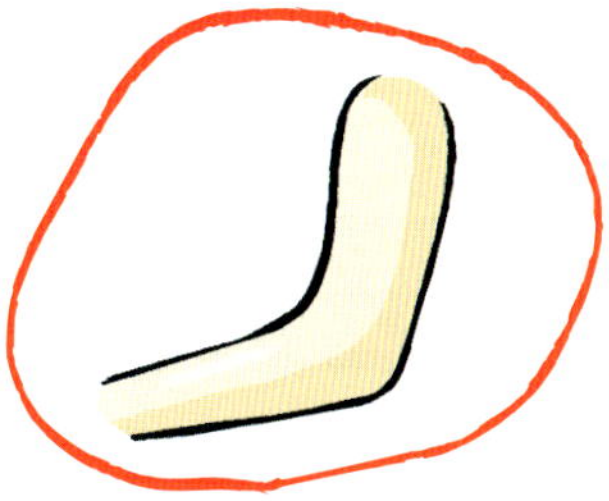

b

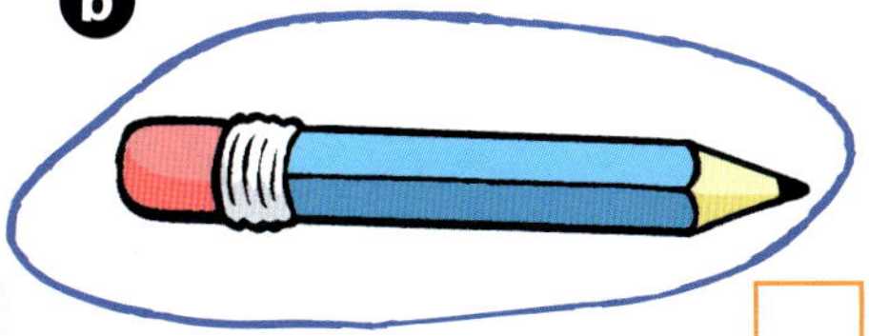

c

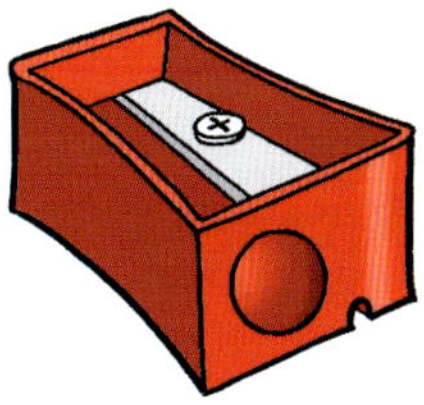

d

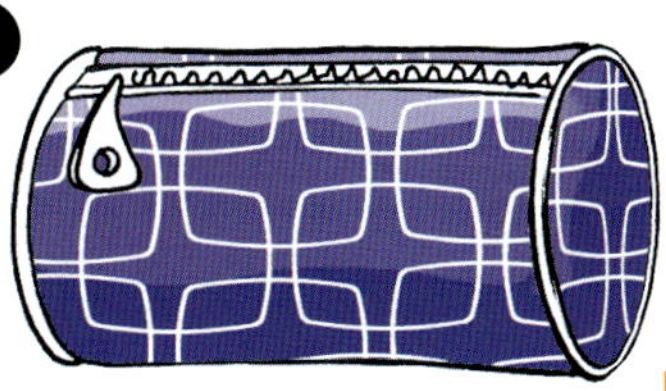

e

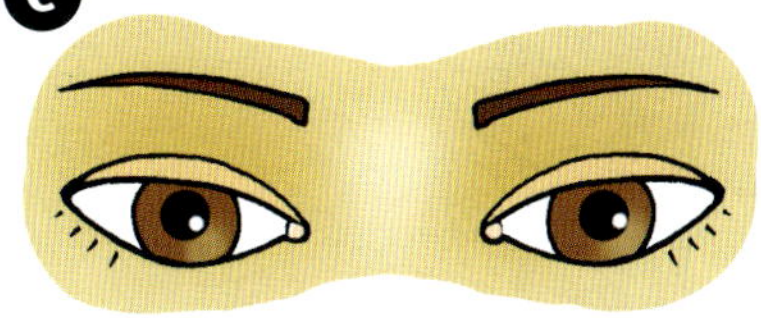

f

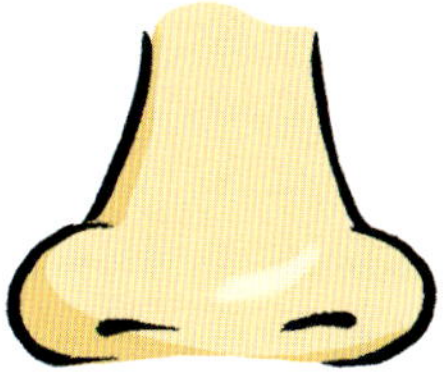

g

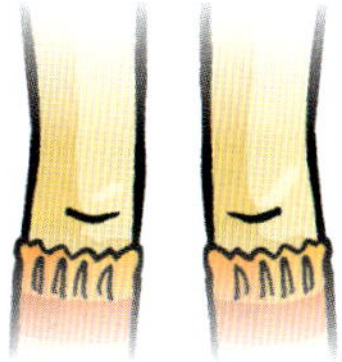

h

i

3 Draw and play *Guess the pictures!*

4 CD1 45 **Listen and point.** **Say.**

5 CD1 46 **Listen and choose.** **Sing your favourite song.**

6 **Think and colour.**

3 Tiger is Lost

Lesson 1 Vocabulary

1 Listen, look and repeat. digital

2 Listen, point and say *Tiger's word chant*.

3 Stick and say. Play *Word or number*.

1 
father

2 
mother

3 
brother

4 
grandmother

5 
grandfather

6 
sister

7 
baby

8 
family

Vocabulary input: *father, mother, brother, grandmother, grandfather, sister, baby, family*

Lesson 2 Story

digital

4 CD2 7 **Listen to the story. Do the action.**

Answer the questions.

Story and language input: *Have you got (Tiger)? Yes, I have./No, I haven't.*

5

6

7

8

Tiger Values

Help your family.

Lesson 3 Story activities

5 CD2 8 Listen and say the missing words.

6 Number the pictures in order. Point and say.

a

b

1

c

d

e

7 CD2 9 Listen and sing *Have you got Tiger?*

Circle who's got Tiger. Trace and colour.

1

2

3

4

5

Lesson 4 Speaking

8 CD2 11 Listen, look and say.

9 Make the cut-out on page 87. Act out the story.

10 Play *Have you got Tiger, Dad?*

Pronunciation: *Granny and Grandad are great!*
Communication: *Have you got (Tiger), (Dad)? Yes, I have./No, I haven't.*

SOCIAL SCIENCE

Different families

Lesson 5 CLIL

11 CD2 12 **Listen, point and say.**

12 CD2 13 **Listen and repeat. Answer the questions.**

PING AND PONG

Content input: different families: *aunt, uncle, cousin, small, big*

SOCIAL SCIENCE

Lesson 6 CLIL

13 CD2 14 Listen and colour red or blue. Repeat.

14 CD2 15 Listen and sing *Some families are big*.
Tick (✔) the family in the song.

1

2

3

4

5

6

15 Talk about your family.

Content and personalisation: *This family is (big). Who's this? This is my (cousin).*

Lesson 7 Unit review

16 CD2 16 Listen, number and repeat. Read and stick.

a

sister

b

c

1

d

e

f

g

h

17 CD2 17 Listen and circle. Look and say.

1

a 

b 

2

a 

b 

3

a 

b 

18 CD2 18 Listen, tick (✓) or cross (✗) and repeat.
Ask and answer.

CLASS CHAT

1 

✗

2 

☐

3 

☐

Learning to LEARN

Go to the Picture Dictionary on page 81.

Kids' Culture 3

1 CD2 19 **Listen, sing and act out a song:** ***The baby wants a mother*.**

video

2 CD2 20 **Listen and number. Draw and say.**

COMPARING CULTURES

a

b

c

Intercultural learning: song: *The baby wants a mother*
Language input: *I live with (my mum and my brother).*

4 Dinner Time

Lesson 1 Vocabulary

1 CD2 23 Listen, look and repeat. digital

2 CD2 24 Listen, point and say *Tiger's word chant*.

3 Stick and say. Play *Word or number*.

1 
peas

2 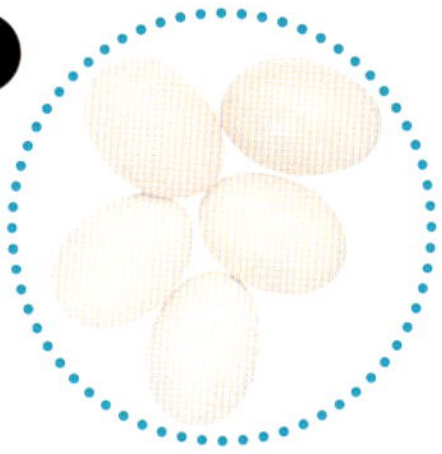
eggs

3 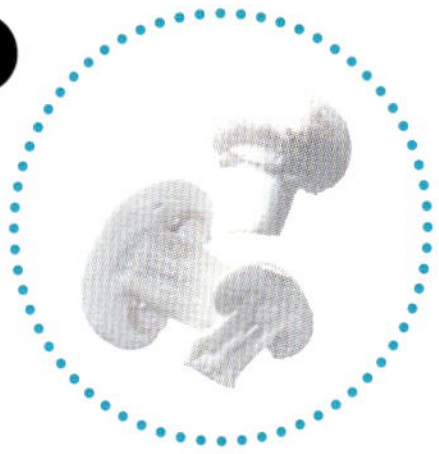
mushrooms

4 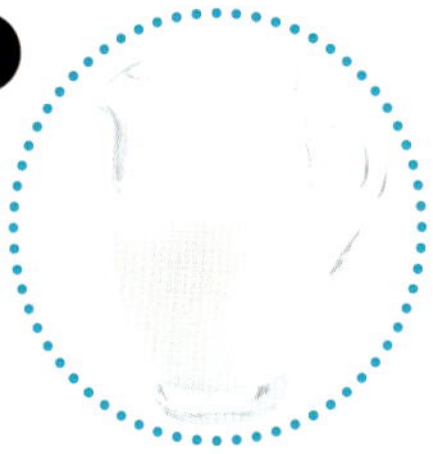
milk

5 
carrots

6 
potatoes

7 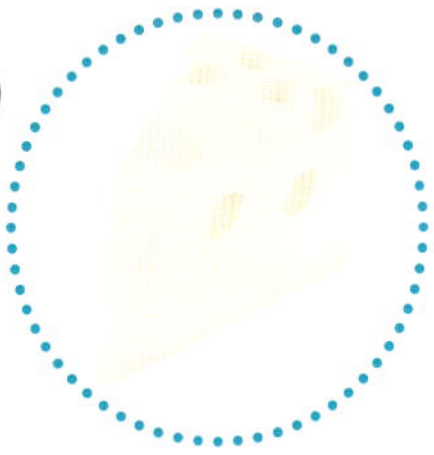
cheese

8 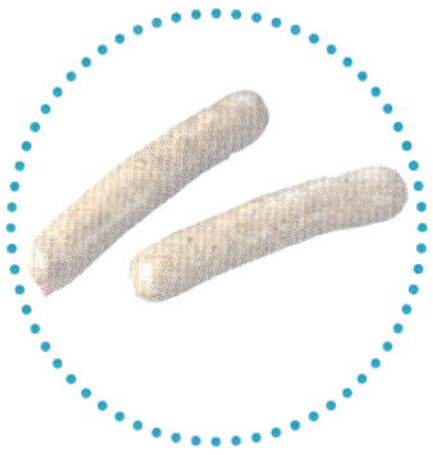
sausages

Vocabulary input: *peas, eggs, mushrooms, milk, carrots, potatoes, cheese, sausages*

Lesson 2 Story

4 Listen to the story. Do the action.

Answer the questions.

Story and language input: *I love/like/don't like (mushrooms). Do you like (cheese)? Yes, I do./No, I don't.*

Tiger Values

Be careful when you're in the kitchen.

Lesson 3 Story activities

5 CD2 26 Listen and say the missing words.

6 CD2 27 Listen, count and trace. Circle the food in the omelette.

1 

2 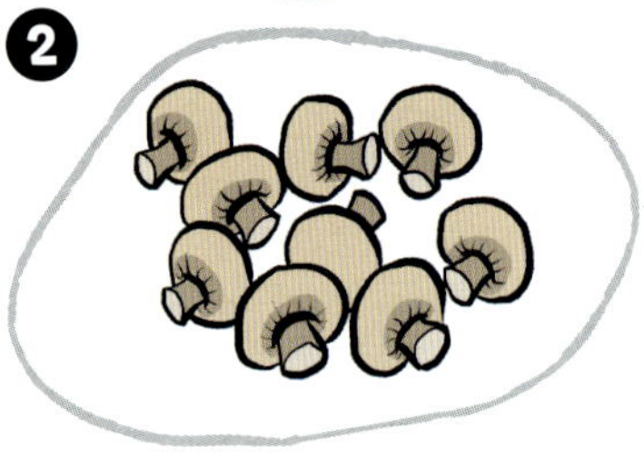

3 

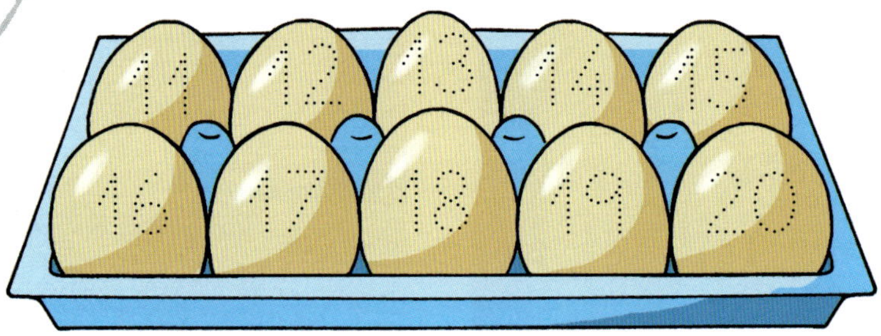

4 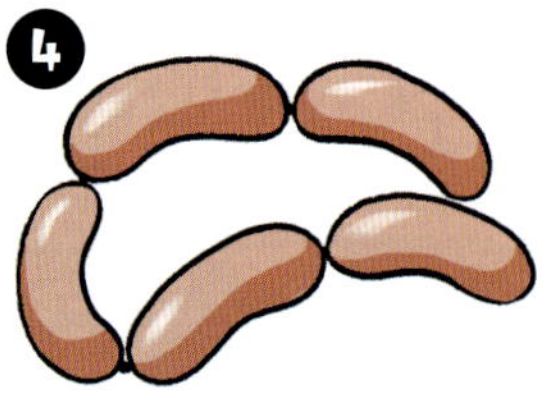

5 

6 

7 CD2 28 Listen and number the pictures in order.

Sing *I don't like sausages*.

a  ☐

b  ☐

c  1

d  6

e  ☐

f  ☐

Lesson 4 Speaking

8 CD2 30 **Listen, look and say.**

9 **Make the cut-out on** **page 89.** **Act out the story.**

10 **Do a role play.**

Pronunciation: *Cheese and peas for me, please!*
Communication: *Do you like (carrots)? Yes, I do./No, I don't. Put (carrots) in the omelette.*

SCIENCE

Food we eat

Lesson 5 CLIL

11 CD2 31 Listen, point and say.

1 2 3 4 5 6

12 CD2 32 Listen and repeat. Answer the questions.

PING AND PONG

Content input: food we eat: *plants, animals, fruit, vegetables, meat, fish*

Lesson 6 CLIL

13 Listen, match and repeat.

14 Listen and point. Sing *Bananas are fruit*.
Tick (✓) the food in the song.

1  ✓

2 

3 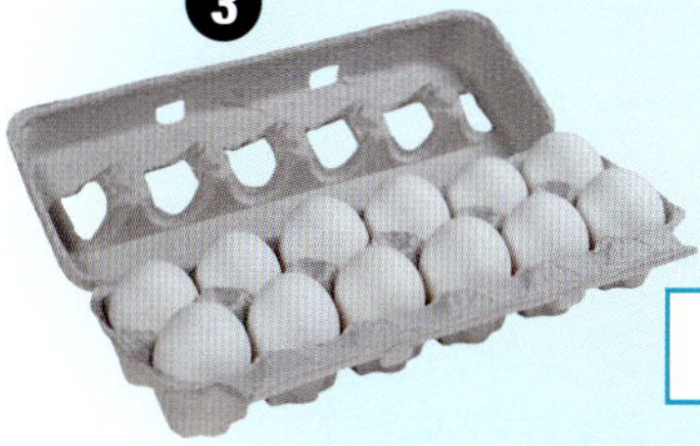

4 

5 

6 

7 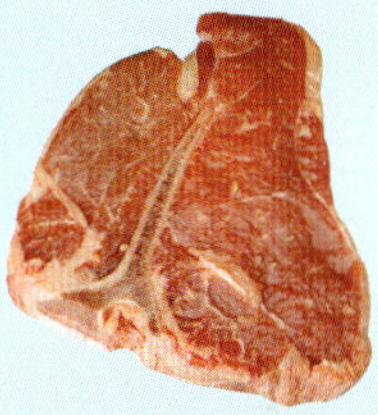

8 

15 Play *I like fish!*

Content and personalisation: *(Bananas) are (fruit). (Bananas) are from (plants). (Beef) is (meat). (Beef) is from (animals). I like/don't like (milk).*

Lesson 7 Unit review

16 CD2 35 Listen, number and repeat. Read and stick.

a

carrots

b

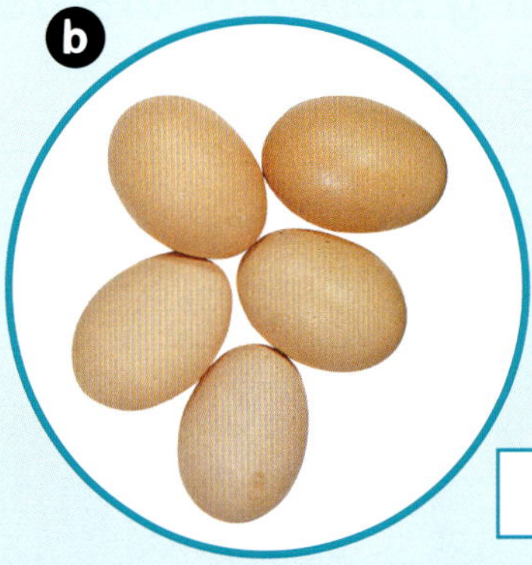

c

d

e

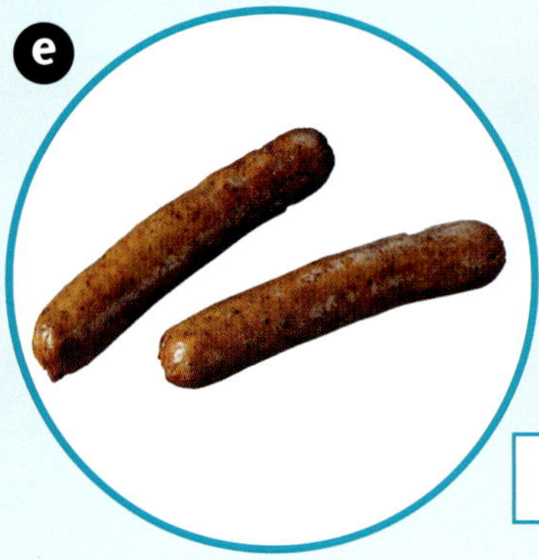

f

g

1

h

17 Look and circle the odd one out. Say.

1    

2   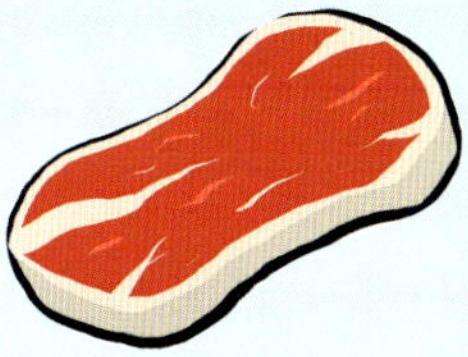 

3 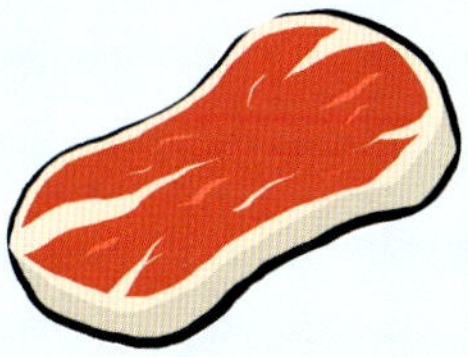   

4   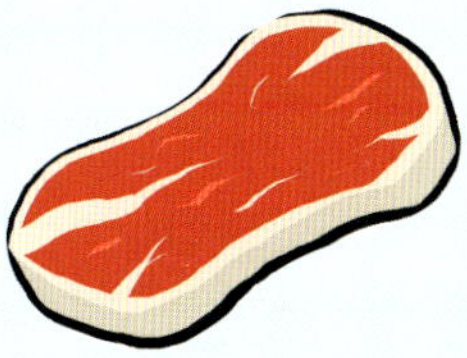 

18 CD2 36 Listen, circle and repeat. Ask and say.

CLASS CHAT

a 11 12 13

b 14 15 16

c 17 18 19

Learning to LEARN

Go to the Picture Dictionary on page 81.

Kids' Culture 4

1 CD2 37 Listen, sing and act out a traditional song: *Ten fat sausages*.

video

2 CD2 38 Listen and number. Draw and say.

COMPARING CULTURES

a

b

c

Intercultural learning: traditional song: *Ten fat sausages*
Language input: *I like (carrots).*

Tiger Review 2

1 Play *Tiger says.*

2 CD2 39 Listen, number and say. Circle red or blue.

a 

b 

c 

d  10

e 

f 

g 

h 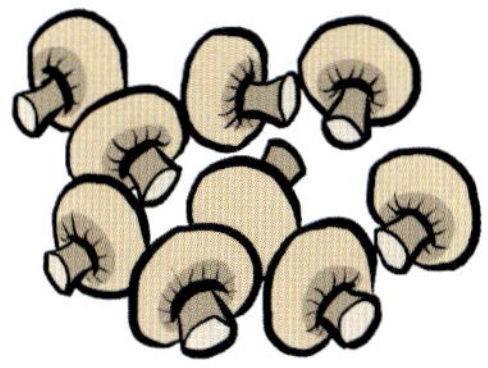

i 

3 Draw and play *Guess the pictures!*

4 CD2 40 **Listen and point.** **Say.**

5 CD2 41 **Listen and choose.** **Sing your favourite song.**

6 **Think and colour.**

5 The Sore Paw

Lesson 1 Vocabulary

1 CD3 5 **Listen, look and repeat.** digital

2 CD3 6 **Listen, point and say** ***Tiger's word chant*****.**

3 **Stick and say. Play** ***Word or number*****.**

1  parrot

2  snake

3  elephant

4  monkey

5  giraffe

6  frog

7  crocodile

8  mouse

Vocabulary input: *parrot, snake, elephant, monkey, giraffe, frog, crocodile, mouse*

Lesson 2 Story

digital

4 CD3 7 Listen to the story. Say *stop!* Answer the questions.

1

2

3

4

Story and language input: *I've got a sore (paw). Can you help me, please? No, sorry. I can't./Yes, of course I can.*

Tiger Values

Be kind to your friends.

Lesson 3 Story activities

5 CD3 8 Listen and say the missing words.

6 Tick (✔) the animals in the story. Circle the animal that helps Tiger.

1 

2  ✔

3 

4 

5 

6 

7 

8 

7 CD3 9 Listen and sing *Can you help me, please?*

Number the pictures in order.

a 

b 

c  1

d 

e 

Lesson 4 Speaking

8 CD3 11 **Listen, look and say.**

9 **Make the cut-out on page 91.** **Act out the story.**

10 **Do a role play.**

Pronunciation: *I've got a mouse and a monkey.* **Communication:** *I've got a sore (mouth). Can you help me, please? No, sorry. I can't./Yes, of course I can.*

How we move

Lesson 5 CLIL

11 CD3 12 Listen and point. Mime and say.

12 CD3 13 Listen and repeat. Answer the questions.

PING AND PONG

Content input: how we move: *walk, run, climb, jump, swim, fly*

Lesson 6 CLIL

13 Listen, number and repeat.

14 Listen and point. Sing *A frog can jump*.
Tick (✔) what you can do.

a

b

c

d

e

f

15 Play *A parrot can fly!*

Content and personalisation: *A (giraffe) can (run). I can (jump). Can you (fly)? Yes, I can./No, I can't.*

Lesson 7 Unit review

16 CD3 16 Listen, number and repeat. Read, stick and write.

a

monkey

monkey

b

c

d

e

f

g

h

1

17 Match and say.

1

2

3

4

5

6

a

b

c

d

e

f

18 CD3 17 Listen, circle and repeat. Ask and answer.

CLASS CHAT

1 🙂 ☹

2 🙂 ☹

3 🙂 ☹

Learning to LEARN

Go to the Picture Dictionary on page 82.

Kids' Culture 5

1 CD3 18 **Listen, say and act out a traditional rhyme:** *Eeny meeny miny moe.*

video

COMPARING CULTURES

2 CD3 19 **Listen and number.** **Draw and say.**

a

b

c

Intercultural learning: traditional rhyme: *Eeny meeny miny moe*
Language input: *I can see a (mouse). It's (brown).*

6 The Missing Skateboard

Lesson 1 Vocabulary

1 CD3 22 Listen, look and repeat. digital

2 CD3 23 Listen, point and say *Tiger's word chant*.

3 Stick and say. Play *Word or number*.

1 
car

2 
doll

3 
bike

4 
scooter

5 
skateboard

6 
kite

7 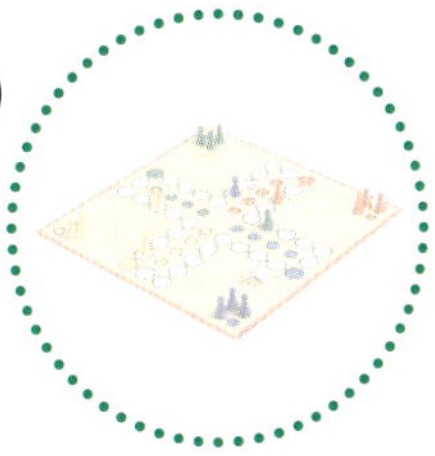
board game

8 
computer game

Vocabulary input: *car, doll, bike, scooter, skateboard, kite, board game, computer game*

Lesson 2 Story

digital

4 CD3 24 **Listen to the story. Say *stop!* Answer the questions.**

STORYTIME

Story and language input: *Where's my (skateboard)? Is it in/on/under the (table)? Yes, it is./No, it isn't.*

Tiger Values

When you play on a skateboard, wear a helmet.

Lesson 3 Story activities

5 Listen and say the missing words.

6 Match the toys to the places in the story. Say.

7 Listen and sing *Where's my skateboard?*

Draw the skateboard.

Lesson 4 Speaking

8 CD3 28 Listen, look and say.

9 Make the cut-out on page 93. Act out the story.

10 Play *Where's my car?*

Pronunciation: *A brown bike and a blue board game.* **Communication:** *The (car) is in/on/under the (book). Where's my (car)? Is it (under) the book? Yes, it is./No, it isn't.*

SCIENCE

Materials

Lesson 5 CLIL

11 CD3 29 Listen, point and say.

12 CD3 30 Listen and repeat. Answer the questions.

PING AND PONG

Content input: materials: *wood, plastic, metal, paper*

Lesson 6 CLIL

SCIENCE

13 CD3 31 Listen, match and repeat.

14 CD3 32 Listen and point. Sing *Materials are fantastic!*
Tick (✓) the objects in the song.

1  ☐

2  ☐

3  ☐

4  ☐

a 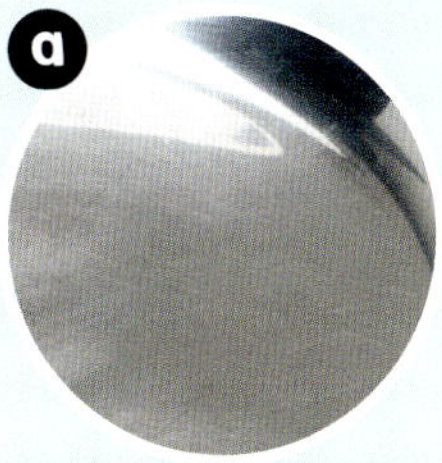

b 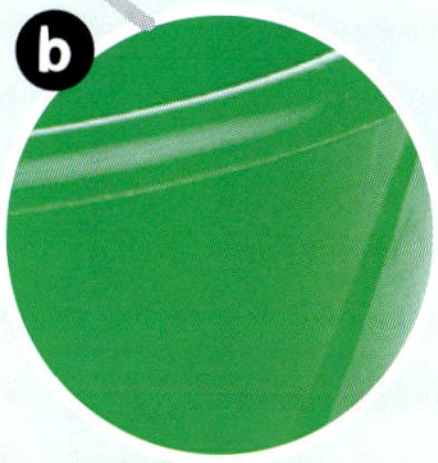

c 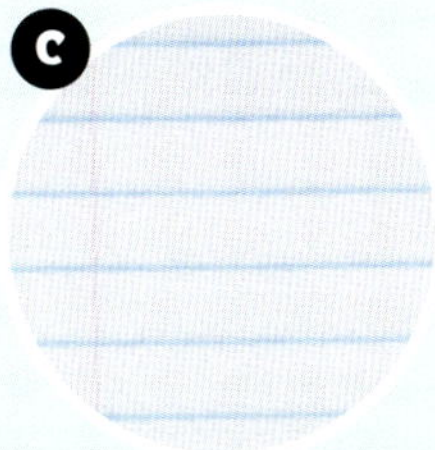

d 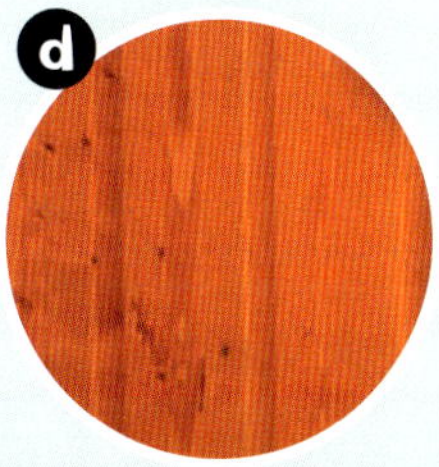

5  ✓

6  ☐

7  ☐

OVER TO YOU

15 Talk about your things.

Content and personalisation: *My (pencil) is made of (wood).*

Lesson 7 Unit review

16 CD3 33 **Listen, number and repeat. Read, stick and write.**

a

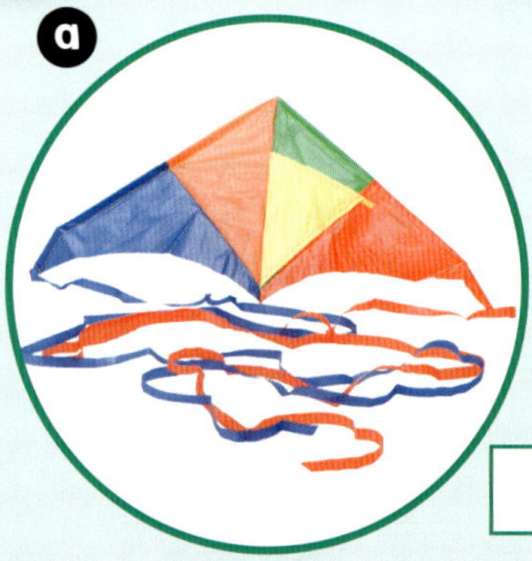

kite

kite

b

1

c

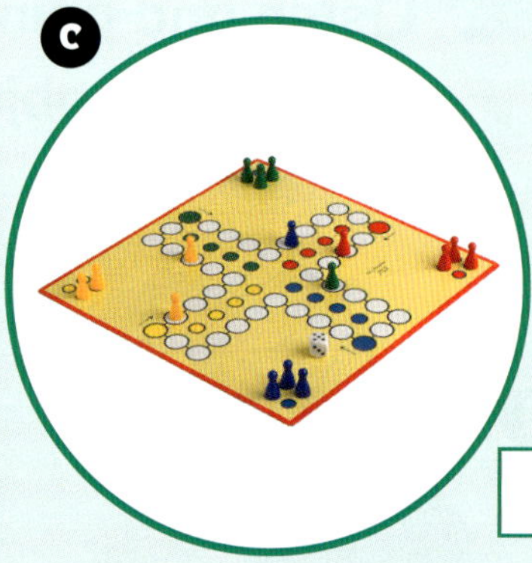

d

e

f

g

h

17 CD3 34 Listen and tick (✓) or cross (✗). Say.

1

2

3

4
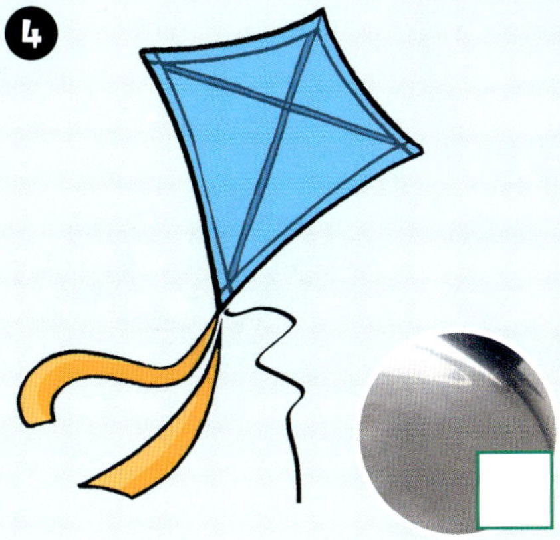

5

6
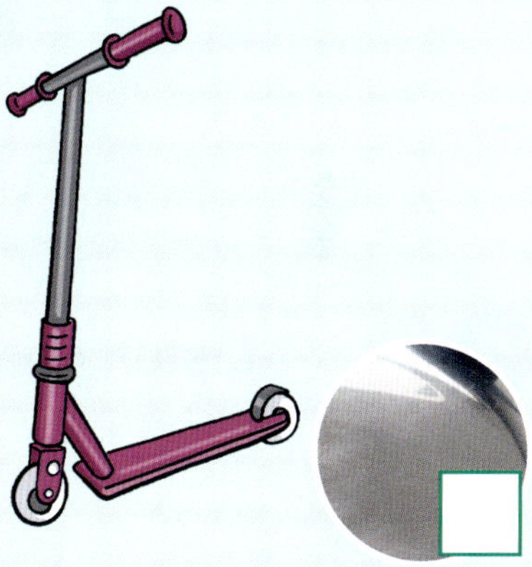

18 CD3 35 Listen, point and repeat. Ask and answer.

Learning to LEARN

Go to the Picture Dictionary on page 82.

Kids' Culture 6

1 CD3 36 **Listen, sing and act out a song:** ***Four great toys in a toy shop*.**

video

2 CD3 37 **Listen and number. Draw and say.**

COMPARING CULTURES

a

b

c

Intercultural learning: song: *Four great toys in a toy shop*
Language input: *In the holidays, I play with my (bike).*

Tiger Review 3

1 Play *Tiger says*.

2 CD3 38 Listen, number and say. Circle red or blue.

a

b
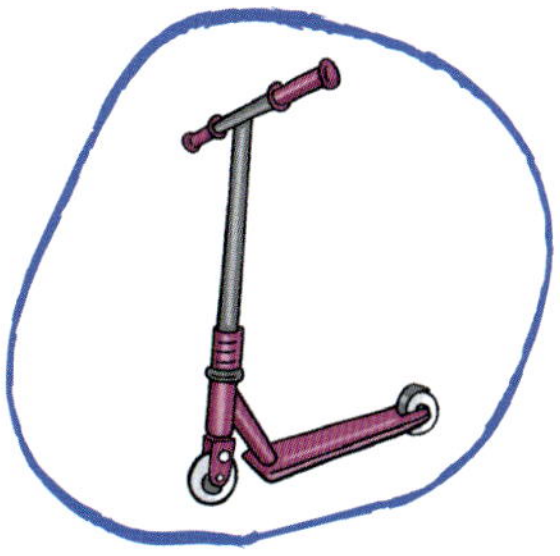

c
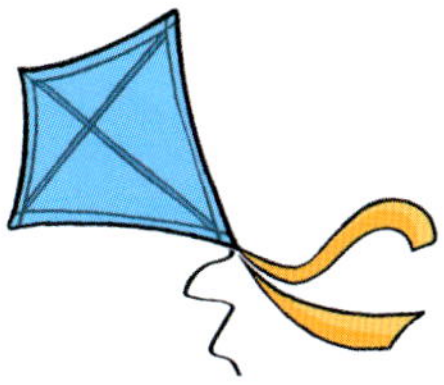

d

e

f

g

h

i

3 Draw and play *Guess the pictures!*

4 CD3 39 Listen and point. Say.

5 CD3 40 Listen and choose. Sing your favourite song.

6 Think and colour.

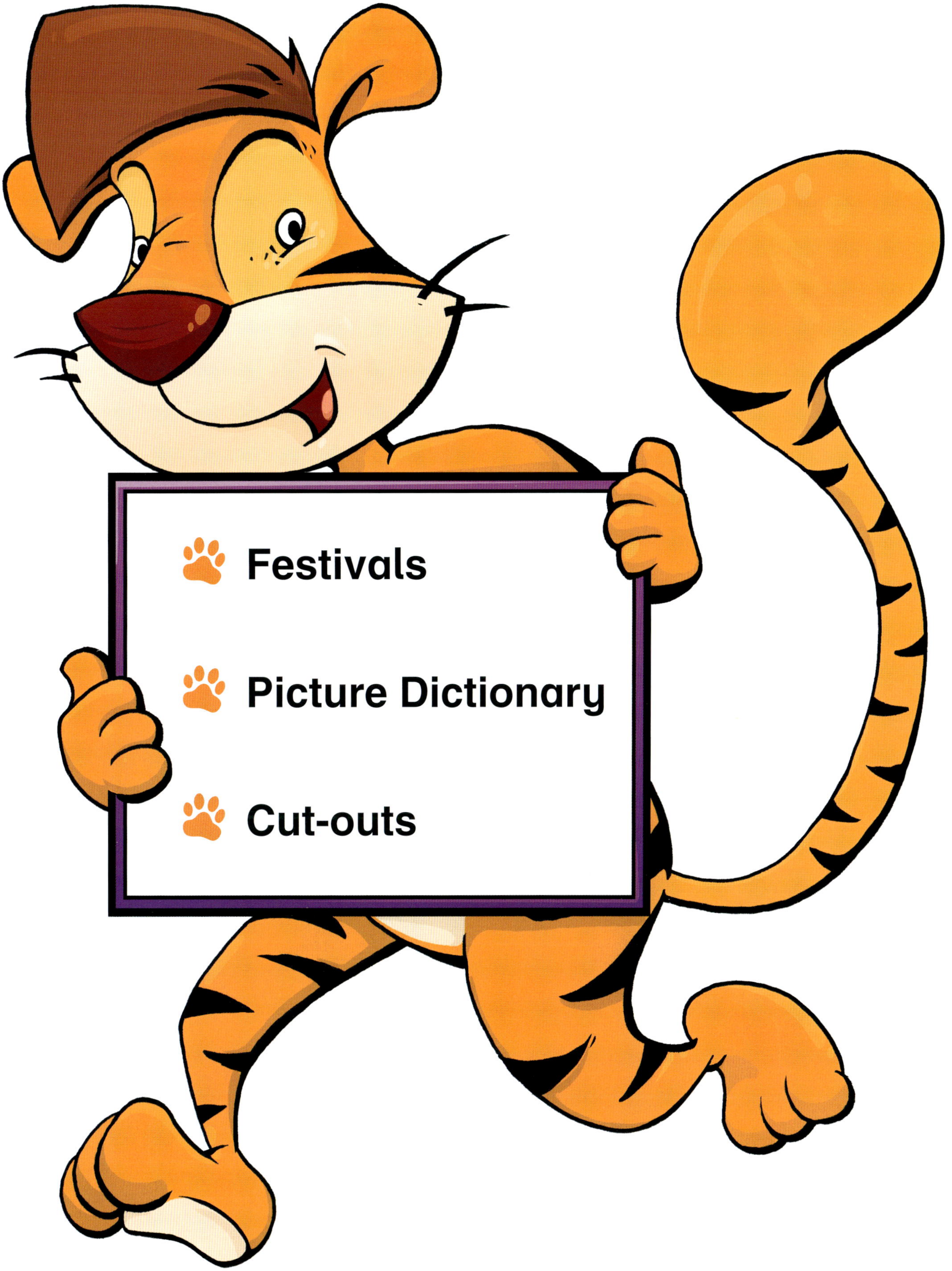
Festivals
Picture Dictionary
Cut-outs

Mother's Day

1 CD4 1 **Listen and point.** **Mime and say.**

1 

2 

3 

4 

5 

2 CD4 2 **Listen and find.** **Sing *Happy Mother's Day!***

Vocabulary input: *basket, bracelet, card, flower, present*

3 Count and write.

a  2

b 

c 

d 

e 

4 CD4 3 Listen, match and repeat.

1 

2 

3 

a 

b 

c 

5 Make a paper basket (TB, p156).

Do a role play.

Communication: *Have you got (a basket?) Yes, I have. I've got (a yellow basket). Happy Mother's Day!*

Father's Day

1 Listen and point. Mime and say.

1

2

3

4

5

2 Listen and find. Say the *Happy Father's Day chant!*

Vocabulary input: *book, cake, football, hat, tie*

3 Look and draw. Say.

1 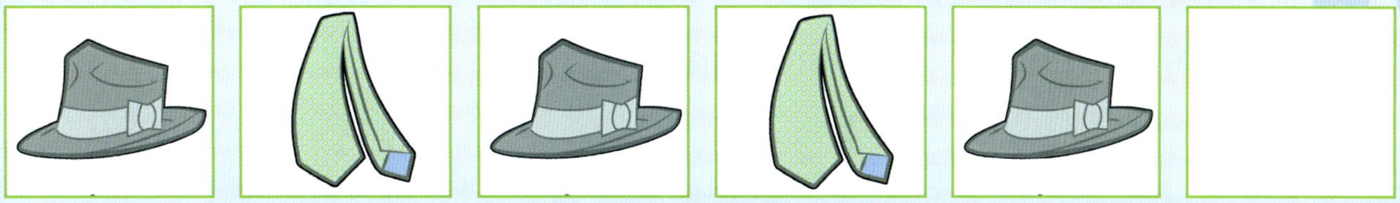

2 

3 

4 CD4 6 Listen, match and repeat.

1  2  3 

a  b  c 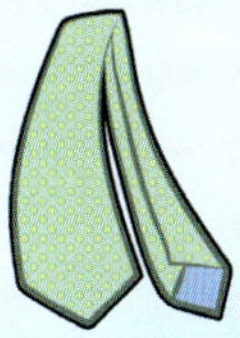

5 Make a Father's Day present (TB, p157). Do a role play.

Communication: *I've got a present. It's for my dad. What is it? It's a (football). Happy Father's Day!*

Teacher's Day

1 CD4 7 **Listen and point.** **Mime and say.**

1

2

3

4

5

2 CD4 8 **Listen and find.** **Say the** ***Happy Teacher's Day chant*****.**

Vocabulary input: *bag, mug, plant, sunflower, T-shirt*

3 Count and write.

a

b

c

4 CD4 9 Listen, match and repeat.

1

2

3

a

b

c

5 Make a paper sunflower (TB, p158).

Do a role play.

Communication: *What's your name? Have you got (a sunflower)? Yes, I have. Happy Teacher's Day!*

Picture Dictionary

Unit 1

bag

crayon

pen

pencil

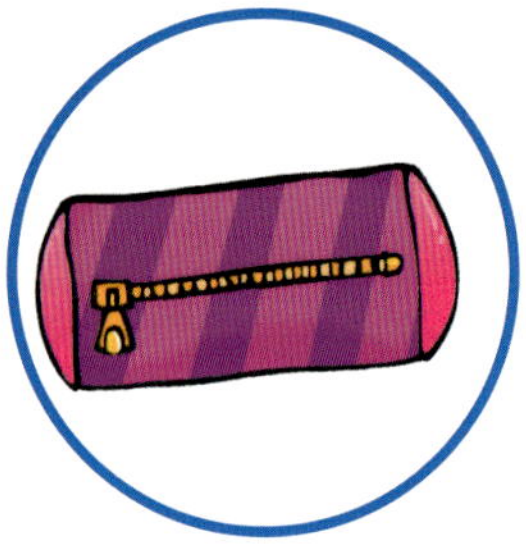
pencil case

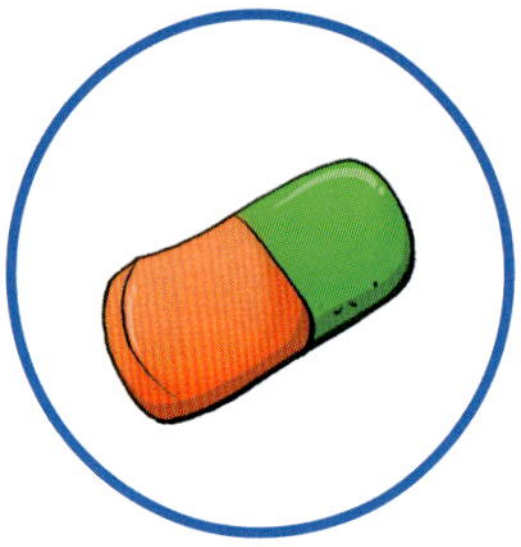
rubber

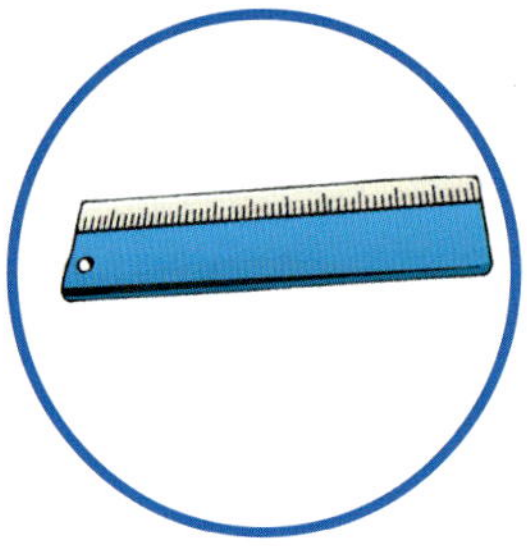
ruler

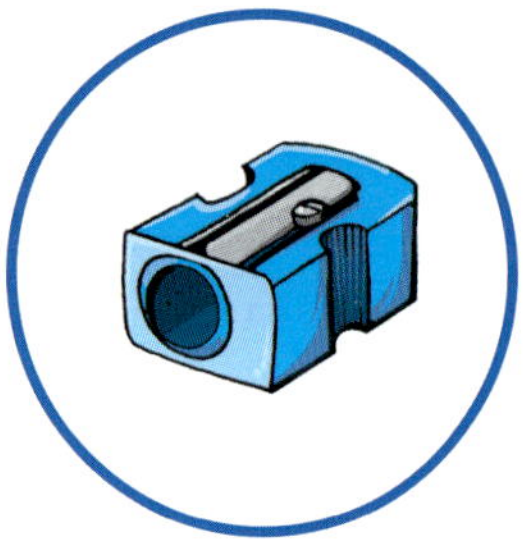
sharpener

Unit 2

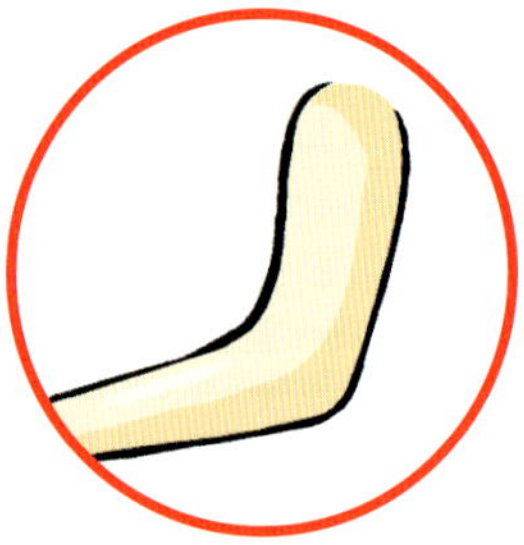
arms

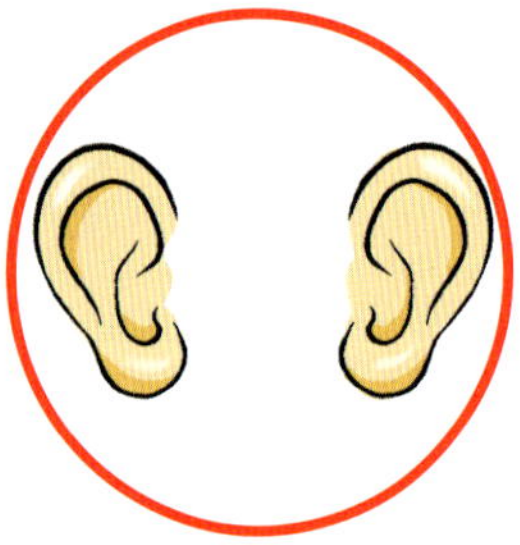
ears

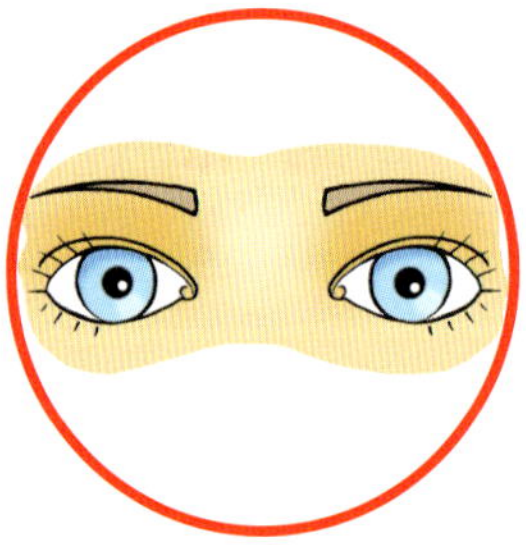
eyes

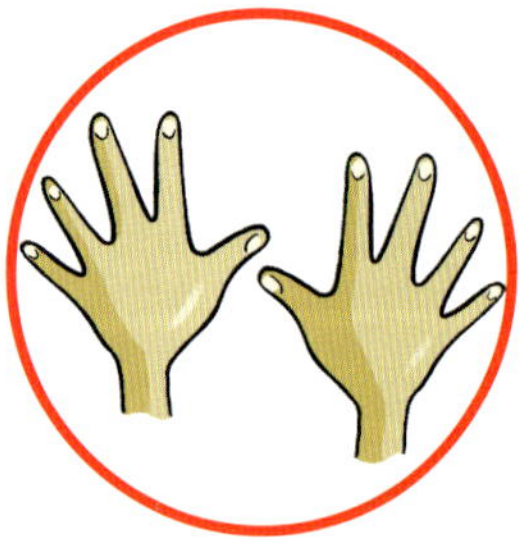
hands

head

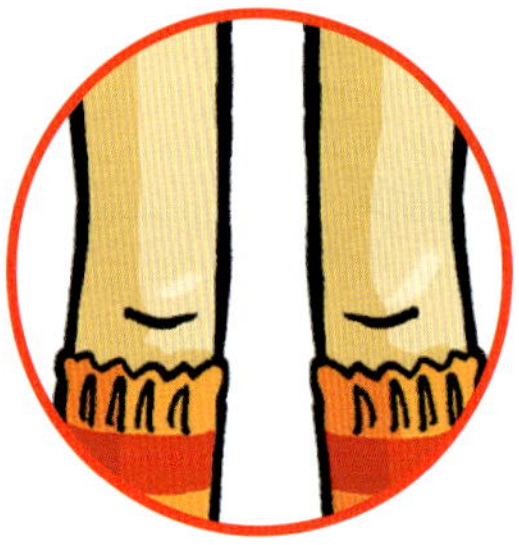
legs

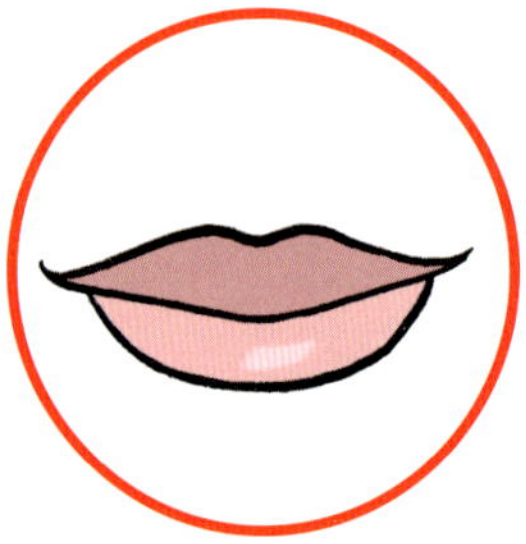
mouth

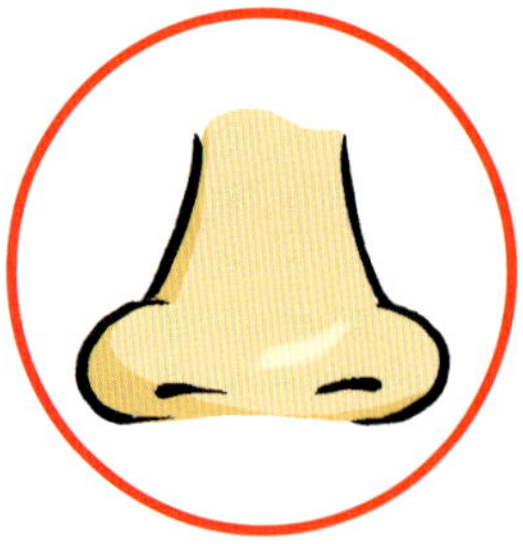
nose

Unit 3

baby

brother

family

father

grandfather

grandmother

mother

sister

Unit 4

carrots

cheese

eggs

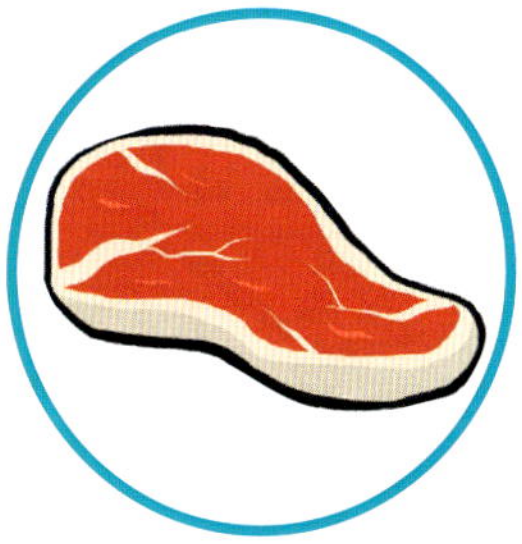

beef

milk

peas

potatoes

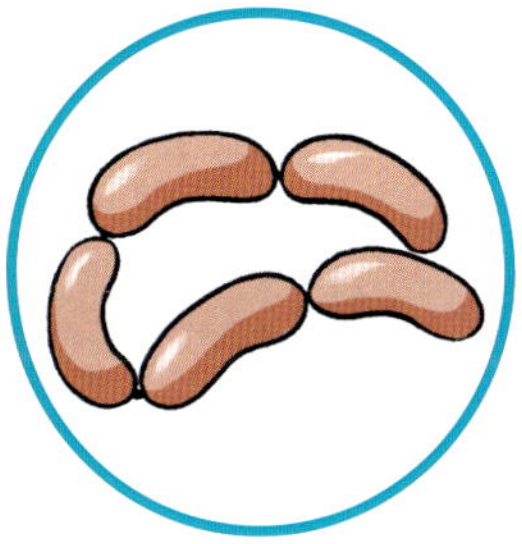

sausages

Unit 5

Unit 6

1

Lesson 4 Make the supermarket basket and classroom objects. Act out the story.

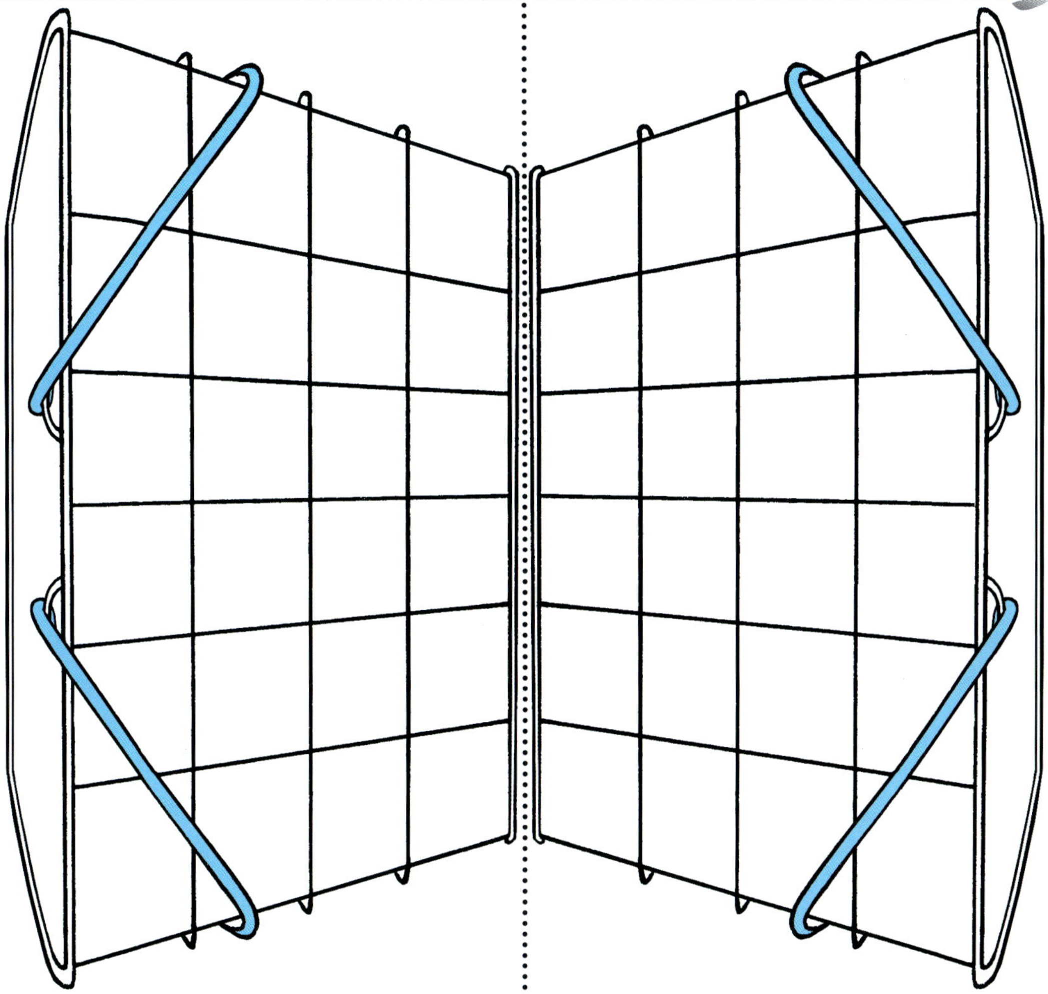

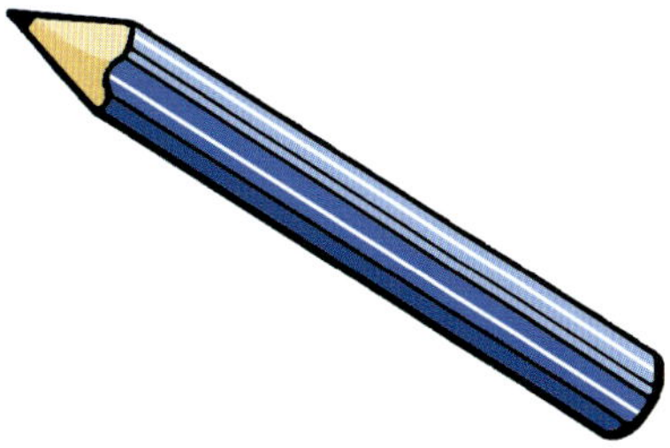

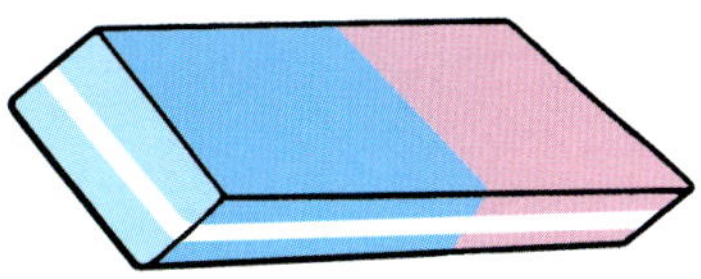

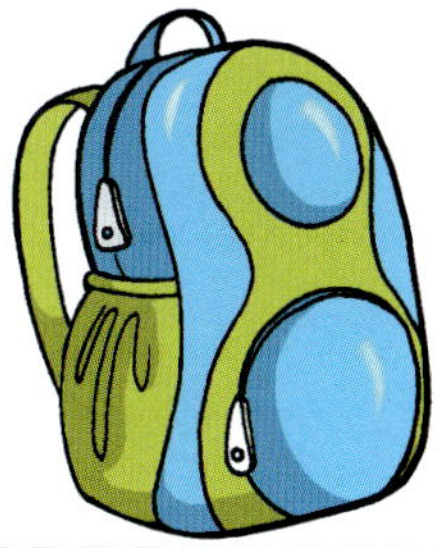

2 Lesson 4 Make the gingerbread man puppet. Act out the story.

3 Lesson 4 Make the family cards. Act out the story.

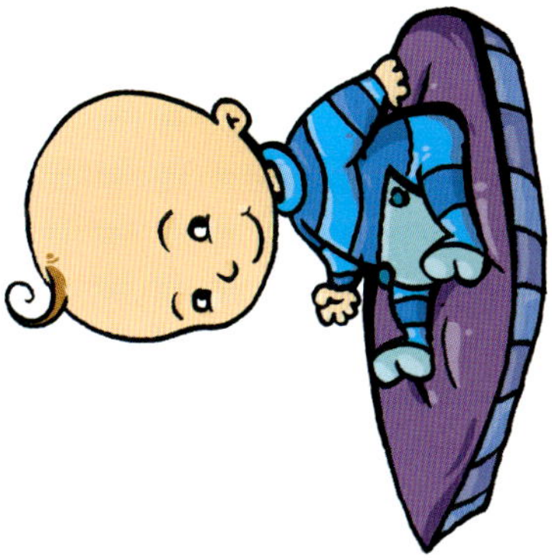

Lesson 4 Make the omelette and the food. Act out the story.

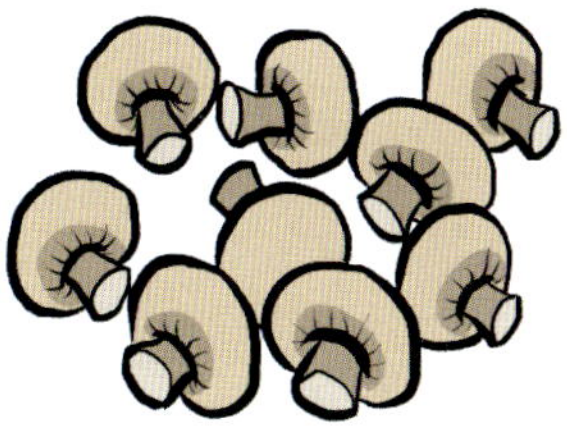

5 Lesson 4 Make the animals. Act out the story.

6 Lesson 4 Make the toy cards. Act out the story.

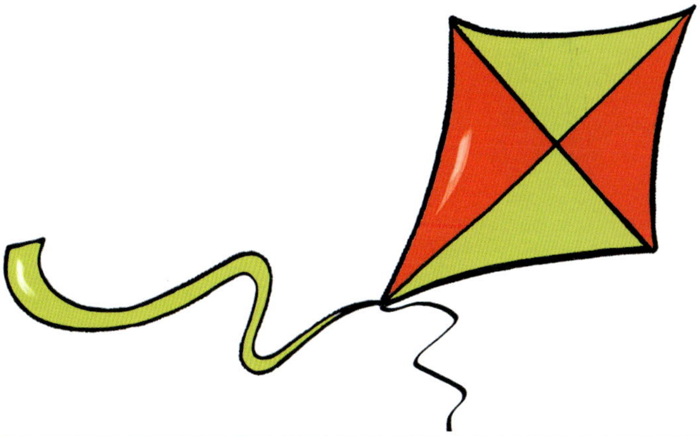

Macmillan Education
4 Crinan Street
London N1 9XW
A division of Springer Nature Limited

Companies and representatives throughout the world

ISBN 978-0-230-48356-9
Pack ISBN 978-0-230-48390-3

This edition published 2015
First edition entitled "Tiger Tales" published 2013 by Springer Nature Limited

Original design by Blooberry Design Ltd
Page make-up by Andrew Magee Design Ltd
Illustrated by Rodrigo Folgueira, Tony Forbes, Kelly Kennedy, Jan McCafferty, Anthony Rule and Jo Taylor
Cover design by Astwood Design Consultancy
Cover illustration by Rodrigo Folgueira
Cover images provided by BrandX; Corbis; Getty, Getty/American Images Inc, Getty/Stephen Dalton; Macmillan Publishers Ltd/Stuart Cox; Stockbyte
Songs produced and arranged by Tom, Dick and Debbie Productions
Recordings produced and arranged by RBA Productions
Picture research by Victoria Gaunt

Authors' acknowledgments
We would like to thank everyone at Macmillan Education in the UK and in Spain who has helped us in the development and the production of these materials. We would also like to thank all the teachers who have taken time to read, pilot and give feedback at every stage of writing the course. Special thanks from Carol to Alan, Jamie and Hannah for their encouragement and support. Special thanks from Mark to Carlos for his patience and understanding.

Acknowledgments
The publishers would like to thank the following teachers:
Ana I. Martín Sierra, CEIP San Sebastián, San Sebastián de los Reyes, Madrid; Ana Mª Muñoz Jacinto, CEIP El Algarrobillo, Valencina de la Concepción, Sevilla; Ángel Martínez Tofé,CEIP Escultor Vicente Ochoa, Logroño, La Rioja; Anna Lorente Clemente, Escola Miquel Martí i Pol, Sant Feliu de Llobregat, Barcelona; Bibiana Comas Planàs, Escola Mallorca, Barcelona; Juana María Torres Medina, CEIP Virgen de Valderrabé, Algete, Madrid; Julia Selma Monedero, CEIP José García Planells, Manises, Valencia; Julie-Ann Eckroth Engelter, CEIP El Tejar, Majadahonda, Madrid; María Ques Jordà, CEIP Son Oliva, Palma de Mallorca, Baleares; Mª Cruz Corrales Fernández, CEIP Santísimo Cristo de la Salud, Hervás, Cáceres; Maripi Arriaga Aznar, CEIP Gerbert d'Orlhac, Sant Cugat del Vallès, Barcelona; Marta Civera Sanfélix, Colegio Sagrado Corazón, Mislata, Valencia; Rafael Aguayo Villamor, Landauri Ikastola, Vitoria-Gasteiz, Álava; Sandra Freire Molina, Colegio La Purísima, Orense; Silvia Cebollada Soriano, CEIP El Tejar, Majadahonda, Madrid; Sylvia Frei Salcedo, CEIP La Cañada, Olías, Málaga.
The authors and publishers would like to thank the following for permission to reproduce their photographs:
Alamy/Peter Banos pp17(5), 24(d), Alamy/Corbis Bridge p53(1), Alamy/ National Geographic Image Collection p56(3), Alamy / Fancy p19(1), Alamy/Simon C Ford p6(d), Alamy/fotoshoot p6(e), Alamy/lan Francis pp66(1), 67(d), 69(1, 3), Alamy/imagebroker p35(br), Alamy/CW; Images pp17(2), 24(a), Alamy/Tetra Images p57(1), Alamy/LJSphotography p78(5), Alamy/NordicImages pp61(3), 68(b), Alamy/M Perris p60(c), Alamy/Purestock p9(r), Alamy/ Laurens Smak pp17(3), 24(h); **Bananastock** pp4, 12(2), 26(a, c). 29(1, 4,7) 31(1, r), 34(2), 35(4), 36(b, d, f) 38(a), 39(7), 41(1), 56(1), 56(2), 56(4), 67(6); **Brand X** p74 (d), pp76 (1, 2, 3, 4,), 12(1), 34(1), 39(6), 46(e), 51(1), 58(d), 76(1, 2, 3, 4), 78(r); **COMSTOCK IMAGES** pp22(5),39(5), 46(d), 67(5); **Corbis** pp34(3),51(7), 58(b),76(4),78(1), Corbis/Steve Cole/Anyone/amanaimages pp15, 25,37, 47, 59, 69(class chat), Corbis/DLILLC p57(c), Corbis/Rachel Frank p67(7), Corbis/Charles Gullung p38(b), Corbis/Streetfly Studio/JR Garvey/Blend Images p67(1), Corbis/Ronnie Kaufman/ Larry Hirshowitz/Biend Images p41(r), Corbis/Kid Stock/Biend Images p70(b), CorbisNstock LLC/Tetra Images pp74(2),75(b), Corbis/Inspirestock p13(e), Corbis/Darren Kemper pp29(5),36(g), Corbis/Kidstock p13(b), Corbis/Lawrence Manning pp66(3),67(a), 69(4), Corbis/George McCarthy p60(a), Corbis/Wojtek Kalinowski Photography pp74(5), 75(e), Corbis/ Leah Warkentin/Design Pies p8, CorbisNstock LLC/Tetra Images pp74(2), 75(b); **Digitalstock** pp51(6),58(e); Eyewire/Getty Images p78(3), **Fancy** pp45(1ettice, cows); **FLPA**/Neil Bowman p57(a); **Fotolia**/Pavel Losevsky p23(b), Fotolia/pressmaster pp26(t); **Getty** pp7(1, 3, 5, 8), 14(d, c, e, h), 22(2, 3), 39(7), 39(1, 2, 3, 8), 44(1r, 3, 4), 46(a, b, f, h), 45(1), 51(2, 3, 4), 56(5), 58(a, g, h), 66(4), 67(c), 69(2), Getty Images pp61(4), 68(e, h), Getty Images/Rubberbaii/Mark Andersen pp74(1), 75(a), Getty Images/nathan blaney p67(2), Getty Images/Phil Boor man p13(a), Getty Images/Streetfly Studio/JR Carvey p21(br), Getty Images/Creative Crop pp61(5), 68(f), Getty Images/Stephen Dalton p57(e), Getty Images/Cultura/Nick Daly p34(4), Getty Images/ Elliot, Elliot pp17(4), 24(f), Getty Images/MacGregor & Gordon p53(r),Getty Images/Steve Gorton pp17(6), 24(g), Getty Images/ Tim Hall p45(br), Getty Images/American Images Inc. p78(2) Getty Images/Jupiterimages p35(1), Getty Images/KidStock p6(b), Getty Images/Darling Kindersley p37(2), Getty Images/Dave King pp61(2), 66(2), 67(b), 68(e),69(5), Getty Images/Nature Picture Library p60(b), Getty Images/Science Photo Library p23(c), Getty Images/Martin Lof/ANYONE p12(4), Getty Images/Don Mason pp74(b), 75(a), Getty Images/MIXA p55(br), Getty Images/Thomas Northcut pp17(7), 24(e), 23(e), Getty Images/Photoconcepts p6(c), Getty Images/Photodisc p76, Getty Images/B2M Productions p70(c), Getty Images/Peter Schoen p57(b), Getty Images/Howard Shooter pp61(8), 68(d), Getty Images/Paul Simcock p26(b), Getty Images/Steve Sparrow p6(f), Getty Images/ Stockbyte pp76(5), Getty Images/Image Source p19(r), Getty Images/ Arthur Tilley p13(d), Getty Images/Reinhard DirscheriNisuals Unlimited, Inc. p57(f), Getty Images/Digital Vision p16(b); **Glow Images**/ Blend RF p34(5), Glow mages/Stockbroker p6(a); **Image Source** 46(g), 76(3), 78(4); **ImageSource and Getty** p45(7); **JOHN FOXX IMAGES** pp44(cow, sheep), 56(6); **JUPITER** pp23(c), 48(a, b, c); **Macmillan** pp44(6),45(apples), 67(4),MACMILLAN AUSTRALIA pp23(a), 39(4), 46(c), 45(6), MACMILLAN\Paul Bricknell pp7(4, 6, 7), 14(a,b,g), 61(1, 6, 7), 68(a, c, g), 76(1) MACMILLAN\Haddon Davies pp7(2),14(f), MACMILLAN/Rob Judges p78(4)Macmillan/ David Tolley p44(5), MACMILLAN NEW ZEALAND p12(5); **Pathfinder** p67(3); **PHOTOALTO** pp35(2), 45(4), 78(5); **Photodisc** pp22(1), 44(hen), 45(sheep, hen, 3, 8), 51(5, 8), 57(d), 58(c, f), 67(br), 74(4,b), 75(d); Photodisc/Getty pp74(e),78(2);**Photolibrary** p44(11); Rex Features/Monkey Business Images p70 (a), Rex Features/ Denis Clason p12 (3), Rex FeaturesNoisin/Phanie p35(5); **SCIENCE PHOTO LIBRARY** pp17(1), 24(b); **STOCKBYTE** pp13(c), 37(3), 63(r), **STUDIO 8** p22(4); **Superstock**/Blend Images pp16(a),74(3), 75(c), SuperStock!Corbis pp16(c), 63(1), SuperStock/Cultura Limited p76(b), Superstocklimagebroker.net p78(3), SuperStock/ Giow Images p23(br), SuperStock/Design Pies pp17(8), 24(c), SuperStock/Golden/Pixals/Purestock p9(1), SuperStock/ Yuri Arcurs Media/SuperFusion p23(d); **Thinkstock**/Creatas p74(c), Thinkstock/iStock pp74(a), 75, 76(4), 78(1) **Up the Resolution** p45(5).

Author photograph (Carol Read) by Michael Selley

Commissioned photography by Stuart Cox pp10, 13(br), 14(a-h), 15, 16(tc), 21(t), 25, 26(tc), 33, 37(bl), 38(tc), 43, 47(bl), 48(tc), 55(t), 57(br), 60 (tc), 65, 69, 70(tc), 75(br), 77, 79.

Thanks to Raffety, Rico & Sophie.

Thanks to Rymans, Oxford.

Printed and bound in Poland by CGS.

2022 2021 2020 2019 2018
21 20 19 18 17 16 15 14 13 12

Unit 1

rubber | sharpener
bag | pencil case
pencil | pen
ruler

Unit 2

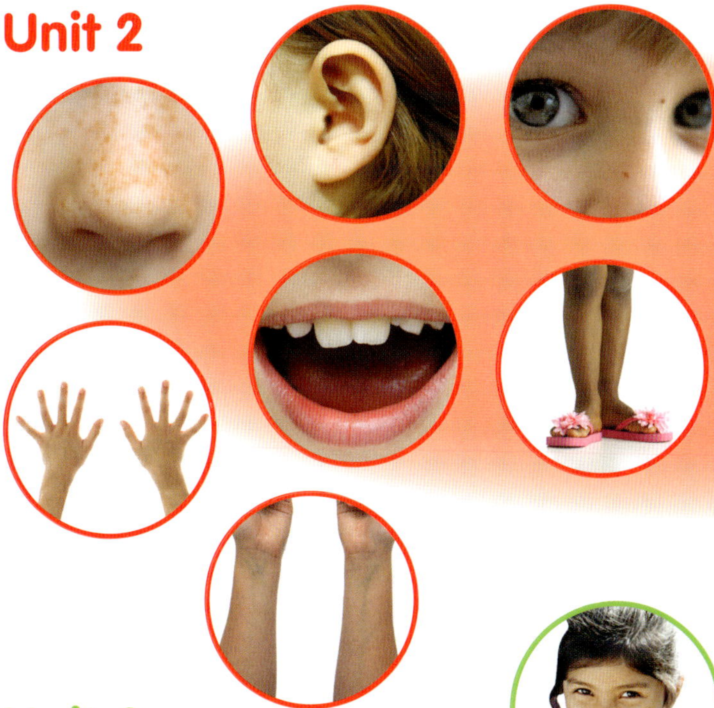

ears | nose
hands | mouth
legs | arms
head

Unit 3

mother | grandmother
baby | family
brother | father
grandfather

Unit 4

cheese	sausages
potatoes	eggs
milk	mushrooms
peas	

Unit 5

elephant	parrot
snake	frog
crocodile	mouse
giraffe	

Unit 6

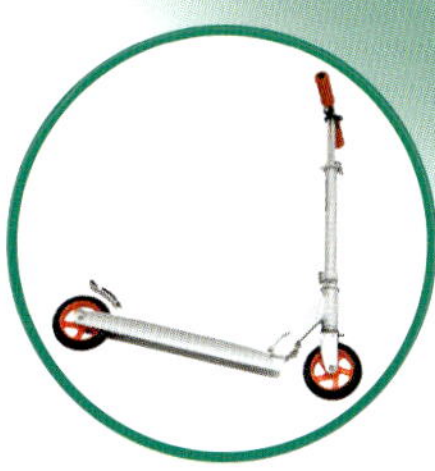

scooter	skateboard
board game	doll
bike	car
computer game	